BLUFF YOUR WAY
IN
SEX

Don and Eve Steel

CENTENNIAL PRESS

About the Authors

Don and Eve Steel know nothing whatever about sex. Their two children were delivered by storks who had been doing what comes naturally with some birds and bees. They are old enough to remember when books about ess-ee-ex were kept under the counter in plain brown wrappers, and they are young enough to remember why.

ISBN 0-8220-2233-8
Copyright © 1990 by Centennial Press

Printed in U.S.A.
All Rights Reserved

Centennial Press, Box 82087, Lincoln, Nebraska 68501
an imprint of Cliffs Notes, Inc.

FOREWORD

Sex in the Age of AIDS

AIDS is the ultimate killjoy. People have to bluff their way through the labyrinth of sex, doing their darndest and hoping for the best, but the AIDS virus is *not* bluffing. It has transformed humanity's favorite sport into Russian roulette. It has even cast a pall over the most blithe aspect of existence – young love.

Sex has always been crazy. It embodies contradictions, for one thing, and arouses passions too violent for weak reason to control. But as crazy as sex was a millenium ago in the Middle Ages, a century ago in the Gay Nineties, a generation ago in the togetherness fifties and the flower-power sixties, or only yesterday in the dull-normal seventies, it's much crazier now.

To write this book, we decided to bone up on the subject (so to speak). We ordered over a hundred sex manuals through inter-library loan, so many that the librarian now gives us the fisheye, convinced that we are disgusting middle-aged sex fiends. Perhaps we are. But the books about sex were a great disappointment. Dull as mud, high-minded, fact-ridden, they could suggest activities that would make Eddie Murphy blush – in language that would induce detumescence on a rutting goat.

Plainly we want something better than that. This isn't an ambitious book, not an attempt to say something authoritative or definitive about sex, not an effort to resolve timeless tensions. Hell no! This is intended as an intelligent entertainment, to beguile an hour or two with an endlessly fascinating subject while providing the bluffer with the raw material for intelligent conversations about sex. As recently as a dozen years ago, a book such as this would have used a few facts from Kinsey, a bit of class from Anaïs Nin, a charge of vulgar energy from Henry Miller, a dash of sophistication from Noel Coward, a bit of spunk from Erica Jong, some irreverence from Thurber, and a dollop of insouciance from Cole Porter. Today one must add an avalanche of caution from C. Everett Koop. This is what the colorful former surgeon general said about sex in the age of AIDS:

> Abstinence is in fact the only option that really prevents sexually transmitted diseases. But children grow up, and, as adults, not too many of them choose to be sexually abstinent all their lives. So what's next? I've advised that the next-best protection is a faithful, monogamous relationship; one in which they have only one continuing sexual partner who is equally faithful. Our job right now is to advise them as follows: that they should be abstinent; if not abstinent, then monogamous; and if not monogamous, then at least supercautious.

The true test of character—for an individual or for a society—is to remain cheerful in adversity. When it comes to sex in the 1990s, we are up to our eyeballs in adversity: AIDS, syphilis, gonorrhea, genital herpes, chlamydia, papilloma, a pandemic of teen pregnancy, a crime wave of rape, kiddy porn and snuff films, hypocrisy from television evangelists, sniggering from the sitcoms, insufferable sex punditry, intractable issues like abortion and gay rights, gender role confusion, a generation of kids lost in the shuffle of musical-bed relationships, a Pill with perilous side effects, and condoms that fail up to half of the time in the real world of bedrooms and back seats. An honest book about sex in the 1990s would be about as aphrodisiacal as an IRS audit.

Sex is still fun and sex is still funny. But that evil genie the AIDS virus is out of the bottle, and even if you're in a so-called low-risk group and use a condom, you still risk getting the virus if you have sex with a stranger. If you're promiscuous, sooner or later your luck will run out. When you lay your body down, you lay your life on the line.

Look, in a very profound way, it's *none of our damn business* what you do or who you do it with. You should glory in your sexuality as an expression of the vitality and fullness of your life. All the pompous sex pundits and all the romantic poets agree about that. A good 1990s image might be this: think of sex in terms of a little nuclear energy—used just right, it'll provide economical power for homes and hospitals and schools, but used carelessly, it'll give us Hiroshima, Nagasaki, Three Mile Island, and Chernobyl.

When it comes to sex, you're bluffing in a game with *very* high stakes.

INTRODUCTION

During the past year, two factors in our civilization have been greatly overemphasized. One is aviation, the other is sex.
—James Thurber and E. B. White, *Is Sex Necessary?*

St. Augustine lamented that he could measure time but didn't know *what it was*. In that respect, sex is like time. We can measure it, but we don't know *what it is*. The fundamental duality of our nature remains mysterious. We can describe sex—our artists, storytellers, and dramatists have been obsessively describing it for aeons. We can analyze it, psychoanalyze it, use it to sell our products, even sell it as a product itself, but we still don't know what it is. Sex is our favorite topic, but when we talk about sex, we're bluffing. For all of our facts, experience, surveys, theories, gossip, scholarship, and what-all, we actually know very little about sex. We can fertilize an ovum in a test tube, engineer a gene in a lab, clone one identical cell from another, but we remain woefully ignorant about sex.

We don't know what sex has to do with love, for example. Something important, we think . . . usually. We don't know why some people who are in love have a rotten time with sex while others who dislike one another have a *marvelous* time with sex. As a society, we have no consensus on what to tell our children about sex (or whether to tell them anything at all), and, as individuals, we spend many of our waking hours (and most of our dreaming hours) wondering whether we should or we shouldn't do this or do that with somebody or other. Whatever we decide to do – or not to do – we're always bluffing because so much that we need to know to make a rational decision is simply unknowable. When it comes to sex, we hardly know what to make of our own urges and emotions, much less how they'll interplay in intimate contact with the fathomless enigma of a lover's heart. Face it: sex is a bluff for creatures like us.

Sex is so important, however, so crucial to our identities, that most of us carry off the bluff with as much panache as we can muster. We do this so well that we sometimes fool ourselves and often foolishly believe that everyone else understands this sex business better than we do. But think about it: would anyone take advice about sex from a funny-looking little middle-aged lady like Dr. Ruth if they had the slightest confidence in their own notions? When it comes to sex, we *all* have our little insecurities, our little anxieties, our little apprehensions, and our large terrors. We worry about rejection, about humiliation, about inadequacy. Even when everything is perfect, even when sexual bliss is joined with true love, still we worry: it can't last, it's too good to last, it never lasts, will I know when it's beginning to lose its perfection?, should I make plans now to be the first to bail out?

Because sex is so important and so personal, and because everyone's bluffing when it comes to sex, this Bluffer's Guide comes complete with a disclaimer: ignore all advice about sex. Sure it's fun to collect advice about sex – provided that it's never taken seriously. The paradox of sex is that every individual is most alone when most intimately enmeshed with another individual who is also most profoundly alone as they try to fuse their bodies into something transcendent. People who give advice about sex can never know what *you're* feeling; however shrewd or worldly-wise the advice-giver, he or she can only guess at what they think you *ought* to be feeling. And few things are less important in either sex or love than some know-it-all who tries to tell you how you *ought* to be feeling. When it comes to sex, you gotta bluff your way through on your own.

Bluff Your Way in Sex isn't going to tell you what to feel – or what to do – or how to do it. If you reflect for a moment, you'll realize that the very idea of advising someone what to feel or how to make love is preposterous. That said, a good bluffer can benefit from many different sorts of ideas and information, just as a good poker player can bluff better after holding a few pat hands. This much is known about sex between consenting adults: things work better if both parties have mutual respect, an appreciation for life's ironies, and impeccable hygiene.

While sex is too complicated for the pithy maxims of self-help literature, its endless ambiguities do make it a fascinating study. Sex can be fun, and funny, and more than a little dangerous. Writing about sex is also a little dangerous – practically anything one says will offend someone: too explicit . . . too vulgar . . . blatantly sexist . . . pruriently pornographic . . . piously puritanical . . . smutty . . . neo-Victorian . . . sinful . . . prudish . . . perverse. How can the reader know whether the authors did enough research to write about sex with authority? (How *did* Dr. Ruth learn all that stuff? Did she *try* it, or does she merely traffic in hearsay?) This guidebook has modest aims. Since writing about sex can be nearly as dangerous as having it and almost as perilous as the celibate lifestyle itself, this handy compendium focuses on the light-hearted aspects of the subject. Before sex, after sex, instead of sex (though only rarely *during* sex—unless you've discovered something *really* kinky), laughter is essential to your emotional well-being. While we quote the great sages of sex and elucidate the masterworks of the erotic canon, we must keep in mind that your sense of humor is more important than your G-spot and your thingamajig put together (even assuming that your G-spot and your thingamajig can be put together in the first place . . . or the second place).

There is, after all, something faintly ridiculous about sex. We do it in undignified postures, if not in downright grotesque positions. While on a Romantic quest for our One True Love, we invariably discover ourselves sexually involved with precisely the last person on earth we ought to be having a relationship with (and more or less completely mystified about how we got involved with this dreadful individual or how to extricate ourselves before madness sets in). Sex is funny in a French farce where everybody's doing it, and sex is funny in *Lysistrata* where nobody's doing it. Just as war is too important to be left to the generals, sex is too important to be left to the psychologists—they take it too seriously.

As you bluff your way in sex, you'll encounter experts who advise you to put your tongue in this place or that place or even (gasp!) the other place, but we recommend that you keep it (for the most part) firmly in cheek.

Your Sexual IQ Test

These questions will test your sexual acumen. You may look for the answers on page 100. Don't worry, even if you don't pass the test, you'll still get to keep your sexual driver's license (or learner's permit, as the case may be).

1. Which of the following is taboo on the first date?
   A. kissing
   B. having sex
   C. having oral sex
   D. having anal sex
   E. picking up the tab

2. Which of the following is the most fun?
   A. fornication
   B. copulation
   C. intercourse
   D. coitus
   E. schtupping

3. The worst thing that can happen to you the first time you try it is:
   A. embarrassment
   B. pregnancy
   C. AIDS
   D. eternal damnation
   E. being caught in the act by your mother

4. Auto-eroticism is:
   A. doing it in your car
   B. doing it *to* your car
   C. doing it with a robot
   D. doing it in Detroit
   E. doing it with Otto

5. What do you think Richard Nixon and Rob Lowe talk about?
   A. sex
   B. lies
   C. videotape
   D. audiotape
   E. deleted expletives

6. Which of the following had the strangest sexual peccadillos?
   A. Warren G(amaliel) Harding
   B. FDR
   C. J. Edgar Hoover
   D. JFK
   E. Gary Hart

7. Which of the following is the handy prophylactic device?*
   A. condo
   B. condor
   C. candor
   D. condyle
   E. condom
   F. conundrum

---

*If you don't know the difference between a condom and a condor, you shouldn't hang around either singles bars or high cliffs in California.

8. Which of the following is a sexually transmitted disease?
   A. diarrhea
   B. logorrhea
   C. gonorrhea
   D. northkorea
   E. all of the above

9. Which is your favorite kind of foreplay?
   A. nuzzling
   B. canoodling
   C. whispering sweet nothings
   D. full-combat karate
   E. Super Mario Brothers

10. You think your sex organs are:
   A. too large
   B. too small
   C. too few
   D. funny-looking
   E. falling into desuetude
   F. clairvoyant

11. This is:
   A. an elephant
   B. a naughty drawing
   C. an interuterine device
   D. proof of Boyle's Law
   E. an early Egyptian sundial
   F. the guy behind you on this morning's bus

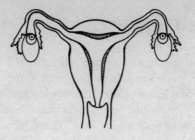

12. This is:
    A. a diagram of the female reproductive system
    B. an aerial view of an off-ramp in Van Nuys
    C. an x-ray of the Maltese falcon
    D. a marine life form that breeds only in the Sea of Cortez
    E. all of the above

MATCHING TEST

A. pudenda   ____ guys who work on boats
B. clitoris   ____ opposite of aftskin
C. semen   ____ meteorologist
D. climacteric   ____ variety of begonia
E. foreskin   ____ Prime Minister of Greece

If you still think there might be correct answers to these or any other questions about sex, go ahead and look for page 100. If you realize that sex is too complicated for answers, but still potentially fulfilling and fun, you just might bluff your way through. Remember the maxim: mutual respect, an appreciation for life's ironies, and impeccable hygiene. And now, as they say in show biz, break a leg!

Caveat Emptor

Are you interested in the statistics of sex? The average penis size soft is between three and four inches, while the smallest functioning penis was less than half an inch long when erect and the largest erection was more than a foot long. The vagina is a muscular tube usually between three to five inches in length, but happily (considering what nature calls upon it to do) it's capable of very great expansion.

You want more? During orgasm, a man's heartbeat rate can rise 250 percent above normal. Had enough? We hope so. That kind of stuff is boring as hell.

Virtually every book about sex for the last 60 years has begun with an apology. As Thurber and White noted in 1929, "The country became flooded with books" about sex. That deluge has only worsened since. The first line of Gary F. Kelly's good 1987 book about sex is this: "Another book about SEX! It hardly seems like we need one." But Thurber and White, and Kelly, and all the other apologists go on to explain why their book is different enough to merit your attention.

So what's *our* excuse? What makes *this* book so special? Nothing. Nothing at all. Sex is an infinitely fascinating topic, a source of much pleasure and diversion. While we're not crazy enough to tell you what to do or how to do it, we can provide a few interesting things to think about and talk about. If you can carry on an intelligent conversation about sex, you'll be a more *rara avis* than the Whooping Crane or the California Condor. This book might provide you with the wherewithal for a bright remark or two. For the rest, sex itself is the ultimate in on-the-job training, the original hands-on activity. Beyond the raw material for some sexy small talk, this book can't help much.

Hey, at these prices, you can't expect Masters and Johnson!

A Brieffe Hiftorie of Sexe*

2 Billion B.C. — A molecule of L-amino acid thought itself so wonderful that it became a replicating nucleoprotein. In inventing life, it invented sex. (Or vice versa.)

4004 B.C. — Adam and Eve rediscover sex in the Garden of Eden with that familiar phallic symbol the snake and a forbidden fruit that may well have been the cherry.

390 B.C. — Lais of Corinth was the most dazzling of the Greek *hetaerae* (perhaps we could translate that as a highly cultivated courtesan or geisha — certainly not a whore). She wrote a love manual describing the various positions. Only one new position has been devised since, and that one is when the woman #$%& with her &%$# while the man tries his best to $%#& with his $&%# without falling flat on his $##. This one is attributed to the first chiropractor who created it to drum up business for a fledgling practice.

55 A.D. — With Nero on the Imperial throne, poisoning his relatives and making Romans listen to his singing,

---

*The silly spelling is supposed to put you in the mood for old-fashioned stuff. Of course, some people have no taste for orthographic wit. If you're one of them, that's just tough titty for you!

Juvenal began to write his savage *Satires*. The sexiest stuff is in numbers II, VI, and IX.

130 –The Greek physician Soranus was busy writing. His biography of Hippocrates is our main source of information about him (Soranus wrote biographies of other and perhaps better doctors, but those works didn't survive; maybe doctors should swear a Soranic Oath). Anyway, his book *Gynecology,* humorously referred to in its day as "that book about spreading old wives' tails," includes this method of birth control: as the man ejaculates, the woman holds her breath, then she squats down and sneezes. This technique resulted in a baby boom during the reign of Hadrian.

875 – King Ewen III made the *droit de seigneur* the law of the land in Scotland. This quaint practice allowed the lord of the manor to enjoy every bride before her husband. Since there was no way the peasants could protect themselves against the rapacious nobility, this only codified common practice.

1115 – Pierre Abelard, the great rationalist theologian of his (or perhaps any) age, became a clergyman at Notre Dame cathedral in Paris, where he met Heloise, the dazzling niece of Canon Fulbert. At 17, Heloise was so brilliant that her lunkhead uncle decided she needed the best tutor in the world – Pierre Abelard. Abelard taught Heloise a thing or two, producing a son with a 1960ish name of Astrolabe. Infuriated, Canon Fulbert hired thugs to emasculate Abelard. Even in twelfth-century Paris, sex could be dangerous.

1191 – Enroute to the Holy Land for the First Crusade,

the advance party of Richard the Lion Heart got itself stranded in Marseilles when it spent all its money on women of easy virtue.

1415 – Pope John XXIII was deposed for incest, adultery, and atheism after supposedly rogering two hundred maids, matrons, widows, and nuns.

1536 – The Queen of England was beheaded for adultery. Having created his own religion to get rid of Catherine of Aragon, his first wife, Henry VIII used a more direct expedient to rid himself of Anne Boleyn, his second. Rumor ran that Henry had enjoyed Anne's mother and her sister before taking up with Anne herself; Henry's fifth wife was Anne's cousin Catherine Howard, beheaded by Henry because he was finally fed up with the family (which, for whatever reason, sure must have known what turned old Henry on).

1555 – Paul IV became pope and decreed that the nudes painted by Michelangelo on the ceiling of the Sistine Chapel were obscene. Daniele de Volterra was ordered to paint clothes on them, winning for himself the nickname "Breeches Maker." In 1559, Paul IV created the *Index Librorum Prohibitorum*, a list of books which no Roman Catholic was allowed to read. The 4,000 titles eventually included books by folks like Balzac, Dumas, and Stendhal. A prude like Paul IV made people nostalgic for popes like John XXIII and Alexander VI (the notorious Rodrigo Borgia).

1639 – In a real-life version of *The Scarlet Letter*, Mary Mandame of Plymouth, Massachusetts, was sentenced to wear a badge of shame on her left sleeve at all times because she had sex with an Indian named Tinsin. The New England Puritans got the bright idea for the letter *A* on the breast in 1658 when a law required it to be sewn on the sinner's garments or else branded on the face with a red-hot iron.

1702 – Lord Cornbury became governor of New York and New Jersey. A transvestite, he spent most of his time wearing women's clothing.

1708 – The Queen's Court Bench indicted Edmund Curll for selling *Venus in the Cloister,* a naughty book about nuns.

1750 – *Fanny Hill, or the Memoirs of a Woman of Pleasure,* was published. This novel by John Cleland was an underground classic for two centuries, supposedly for its "literary value." Its literary value is nil. Less than nil.

1770 – Pope Clement XIV began to excommunicate men who castrated boys to preserve their pure soprano voices. Papal choirs continued to use *castrati,* though, so the practice continued. It's rumored to continue to this day.

1777 – The Marquis de Sade's mother finally had him locked up in the Bastille, where his equation of sexual pleasure with inflicting pain could find only literary output. He died in the lunatic asylum in 1814. They knew enough to lock up sexually dangerous people in 1814.

1834 – Sylvester Graham, inventor of the graham cracker, wrote "A Lecture to Young Men on Chastity," a work assuring young men that sex leads to insanity and that every ejaculation shortens life expectancy.

1866 – Dr. Russell Thacker's *Sexual Physiology* repeated the suggestion that sneezing can prevent conception, thereby contributing to a post-Civil War baby boom.

1872 – Samuel Parkinson of London was convicted of selling candy decorated with pictures of people doing it. He was ahead of his time; such confections sell well in London today.

1895 – Paris introduced the striptease. In "Le Coucher d'Yvette," Yvette slowly undressed while ransacking her clothes for a flea.

1900 – Freud wrote *The Interpretation of Dreams*. Psychology began to spoil sex in deadly earnest.

1928 – The Germans published an illustrated encyclopedia of sex, the *Bilder-Lexicon der Erotik*. (You'll recall from the movie *Cabaret* how decadent things were in the latter days of the Weimar Republic.) Hitler came to power in part by promising to restore sexual purity, and you recall where *his* experiment wound up. (Jerry Falwell's 1970s Moral Majority movement was a similar attempt to seize power, but died out for lack of interest.)

1933 – "Le cirque erotique" was popular in (where else?) Paris. Naked women raced around a track on bicycles. (They could have come up with a better idea than that in Davenport, Iowa.)

1946 – Massachusetts Attorney General George Rowell tried to ban Kathleen Winsor's novel *Forever Amber*, which wags have dubbed *Forever Under*.

1953 – The very first Playmate in the very first *Playboy* was Marilyn Monroe in a Tom Kelley photo purportedly from the session that produced her still-popular calendar art.

1964 – The topless look was introduced by fashion designer Rudi Gernreich. To this day, feminists are getting themselves arrested in Rochester, New York, because of the injustice of allowing men to appear in public naked from the waist up – but not women.

1969 – *Penthouse* magazines arrived in the United States with the first mass-marketing of what they call in the trade "split beavers."

1970 – President Nixon called his own Commission of Obscenity and Pornography "morally bankrupt" for urging restraint on any effort to ban explicit materials about sex. In the 80s, President Reagan's commission on the same subject also fizzled – despite being headed up by then-Attorney General Ed Meese (himself later branded as morally bankrupt).

1972 – *Cosmopolitan* published a nude male pinup centerfold featuring Burt Reynolds (almost) in the buff (wearing only his hairpiece). (The British edition featured feminist Germaine Greer's then-husband, Paul de Feu.)

1977 – Sex-enhancing plastic surgery was all the rage. *Vogue* reported over 1,000 operations to realign the clitoris; Dr. F. Brantley Scott of Baylor University in Houston invented a penile-erection device for sex-change operations to surgically transform females into males.

1989 – Television evangelist Jim Bakker was convicted of fraud. He and dozens of other television evangelists had been frauds for years, so his real sin was frisky lewdness with a church secretary. Similarly, evangelist Jimmy Swaggart dramatically told his followers "I have sinned," coincidentally after having been exposed by the press as having "frequented prostitutes."

1990 – Sex was revolutionized with the appearance of the best-selling *Bluff Your Way in Sex*. This Bluffer's Guide made all subsequent sex reasonable, pleasant, and risk-free. Its principles of mutual respect, ironic detachment, and impeccable hygiene were universally adopted.

THE DEFINITION, THE LANGUAGE, AND THE MECHANICS OF SEX

Amoebas at the start
Were not complex.
They tore themselves apart
And started Sex.
—Arthur Guiterman, "Sex"

Defining Sex

People spend so much time talking about sex and writing about sex and singing about sex and dreaming about sex that it ought to be easy to define. Well, it is, and it isn't. The dictionaries and the biology books all assume that sex is about reproduction. This is typical: "**sex.** The state of an individual as determined by its adaptation for a special part in biparental reproduction and modifications of the process."

Many children experience their first sexual frustration when they try to learn about sex from books and then encounter sentences like that.

Here's another definition: "**sex** (seks) *n* 1. either the male or female division of a species, esp. as differentiated with reference to the reproductive functions."

There's that word again—reproduction. Okay, sex has something to do with reproduction. But just think

about the number of times that you've had sex compared to the number of times that you've been a father or mother. In spite of all the babies being born, the percentage of times that sex results in reproduction is statistically insignificant, maybe .0000000000000000000000000000000000000000001 of one tenth of one percent. Virtually everyone having sex is not only uninterested in reproduction but *actively hostile* to the notion. In fact, sex seems only solipsistic, an activity concerned primarily with itself. Anthropologists tell us of tribes which refused to believe that babies were conceived the way modern science insists they are — with so much screwing and so few babies, the link made no sense at all to them; the association defied common sense. Sex was about sex, and babies came willy-nilly from god-only-knows-where; that was their notion.

We moderns, we're much more sophisticated than that. Sort of. We know *how* babies are made, but we don't know why, or why it takes two sexes, or why our species is obsessed with sex every day (make that every minute) instead of just during a mating season. Forget historical and cultural and social factors. We don't even know why there *are* two sexes, much less how they ought to behave. The key questions about sex transcend biology to involve everything from epistemology to hermeneutics. You can spend hours studying biology, epistemology, and hermeneutics, or you can take our word for it — humanity circa 1990 is profoundly ignorant about sex despite all the confident punditry on the subject. We hardly know how to define terms for a reasonable debate.

Why *are* two sexes necessary for reproduction? The

amoeba does all right with just the one. Humanity has always flattered itself that it was the highest of the mortal life forms and that there had to be some very good reason for the bifurcation into male and female. Maybe so. But not necessarily in terms of science. It's by no means obvious that everything nature does is for the best. Here's how Charles Darwin put it: "What a book a devil's chaplain might write on the clumsy, wasteful, blundering, low, and horribly cruel works of nature!" The necessity of two sexes for reproduction may be part of a Divine Plan or it may be a perversely unnecessary quirk of evolutionary accident. In his essay "Big Fish, Little Fish," Stephen Jay Gould puts the matter this way: "We might ask why males exist at all. Why bother with sex if one parent can supply the essential provisioning?" In scientific terms, the answers to that question are tentative.

Whatever sex is, we must approach the subject with a frank recognition of how little we know. This is from the 1948 preface to Dr. Alfred C. Kinsey's pioneering survey *Sexual Behavior in the Human Male*: "As long as sex is dealt with in the current confusion of ignorance and sophistication, denial and indulgence, suppression and stimulation, punishment and exploitation, secrecy and display, it will be associated with a duplicity and indecency that lead neither to intellectual honesty nor human dignity." What a wonderful sentence! Just as true today as the day it was written.

Is there any evidence that American society is dealing with sex in ways that lead to intellectual honesty or human dignity? Not much. Consider the puerility of sex on TV sitcoms, the banality of sex in self-help magazine articles, the inanity of sex in Harlequin

26

romances, the vulgarity of sex in the routines of our most famous stand-up comics, the absurdity of sex in tabloid headlines, the savagery of sex in rape statistics, the sadness of sex in divorce rates, the priggishness of sex in sex education classes in our schools, the meretriciousness of sex in advertising, the falsity of sex in typical Hollywood movies, the hypocrisy of sex in politics, the irrelevance of sex in religion, the confusions about sex in law, the crises about sex in medicine. Clearly, we've overcome some of our puritanical inhibitions, but we're still at least half-daft when it comes to sex.

Sex defies easy definition because sometimes we mean the mechanics of reproduction, and sometimes we mean the cultural anthropology of courtship-cum-child rearing and sometimes we mean the physical aspects of love. Very often we're talking about gender conflict in a society where rapid change is the only constant.

Biology can teach us this much: either sex is incomplete. It takes both sexes to reproduce. How or why this happened, it has profound consequences. Human potential, in either the angelic or demonic directions, requires both masculine and feminine elements. In coming to grips with the opposite sex, we do much more than make reproduction a theoretical possibility. Sex is how we express our nature, and both sexes are necessary to express our complete nature. If we're after more than babies when we have sex, we're also after more than carnal bliss (nice as both babies and carnal bliss can be). We're in quest of a oneness that can be achieved only in the fusion of our duality.

The fundamental fact about sex for our species is a

paradox. The important things to know about sex must be sought in ambiguities, ironies, nuances, and dualities. Some of the truths about sex can be expressed only in poetry and appreciated only by intuition. Virtually all nonfiction about sex consists of poppycock, twaddle, balderdash, hogwash, cant, and trivia. That's just the way it is. Sex is a vast subject, nearly synonymous with life itself, so it takes years to learn, and by the time you learn anything at all, you've become a different person with just as much to learn as when you started.

If it's any consolation, the so-called experts are bluffing. There's no evidence to suggest that the biologists or psychologists or anthropologists or sociologists who pontificate about sex are any better in bed or have happier marriages than ordinary slobs who learned about sex by reading restroom walls.

Having warned you against wisdom about sex, here is some. (This subject is best approached by paradox, after all.) Sex is fun to study (hell, sex is fun just to *think* about). That's a key concept right there – fun. Sex is fun. Sex *ought* to be fun. The Dutch philosopher Johann Huizinga insisted that our species was pompously wrong to call itself *Homo sapiens,* man-the-wise. Judged by our record, wisdom is not our defining characteristic. Huizinga suggested *Homo ludens,* man-the-playful. That's a useful concept to play with. *Bluffing* is a term from play. Sex is a playful aspect of life: we flirt, we tease, we cheat, we score, we win and lose. If we define sex as a game, albeit an important and potentially dangerous game, we'll be reminded that practice and study pay great dividends, and bluffing is a necessary last resort. In the game of sex, the play itself is great sport and the prize is mutual self-realization. (Sometimes, however, a wee one.)

A fatal error is assuming that you win the game of sex by defeating or besting or outscoring your partner. In fact, you and your partner must *both* beat the odds. When you and your partner play the game of sex so well that you manage to beat the odds, there's a name for that: love.

The Language of Sex

Sex is at the core of each of us – as biological animals and as social animals. Language is also central to our individual and cultural identities. These two truisms make the language of sex one of the trickiest propositions imaginable. Most of the talk about sex takes place among a bunch of guys on a hunting trip or a bunch of gals at a bridal shower or a gang of rowdies of both sexes at a local tavern or a gaggle of high school kids showing off for one another at a party after the prom or a slew of sailors on leave in a liberty port, and this talk about sex is conducted in graphic and colorful argot, laced with a lot of words having their dark roots in Anglo-Saxon.

For reasons too complicated to pursue, the *written* language of sex has been less free to avail itself of the colorful terms so common in speech. Thus, even today, the more vulgar Anglo-Saxonisms about sex retain some of their shock value.

The English language is downright schizophrenic when it comes to sex. Most of what appears in print and much of what is spoken about sex is expressed in circumlocutions. It doesn't take a genius to conclude that we wouldn't have developed two fundamentally different languages to describe the same basically simple functions if we weren't of two minds about the subject. Perhaps the best way to think about why we developed two different languages to talk and write about the one subject of sex is to admit to ourselves that modern humanity's confusions about the nature of sexuality amount to mass hysteria sustained over centuries.

It's a commonplace of poetry and psychiatry alike that love drives lovers crazy. That is why people are all bluffing when they write or speak solemnly about sex, as if it might be explained like Boyle's law or Avogadro's number or the Pythagorean theorem or anything else we might all understand and agree upon—if only we would concentrate and think clearly for a few minutes. Sex drives otherwise timid people to frenzies of lust, rampages of jealousy, and abysmal depths of depression. And why does sex do this? Because, when sex is at its best, it lifts us to soaring heights of ecstasy and transports us to realms of scarcely imaginable bliss. Small wonder we have two languages to deal with sex. The stuff is dangerous!

Because sex is so dangerous, it was until recently, like matches, kept out of the hands of children. This was managed in large part by language taboos. Consider the problem facing Edward Gibbon, for example. The great British historian devoted his life to writing the monumental *Decline and Fall of the Roman Empire*, which appeared at the same time as the American Revolution. Gibbon had to describe the antics of Caligula and his ilk, sexual gluttons whose shenanigans were so saucily depicted in *I, Claudius* on PBS that we almost wrote a check during pledge break. Gibbon resorted to erudite subterfuge: he put all the sexy stuff into footnotes—in *Latin!* That way, if his scholarly tome fell into the hands of an impressionable child, he or she could read all the dull passages about Caesar's military campaigns against Vercingetorix but nothing at all about the orgies of Nero and his sybaritic sycophants. The Latin in Gibbon's footnotes was beyond the ken of altar boys or third-year students, but rumors about the material prompted many generations of teenage boys to cram more about the dative and ablative absolute into their brains than they might otherwise have done.

What Gibbon did in his famous footnotes, everyone else did in polite discourse. Custom decreed that people speaking English would use Latinate words to talk or write about sex. This was supposed to protect the young, who presumably didn't know the meaning of the words, and it was supposed to help defuse sex for grownups by keeping it at a distance—as scholarly and abstract and impersonal and scientific and *dull* as possible. That's why sex was—and to some extent still is—described in terms like this: *the act of coitus involves the insertion of the penis erectile into the vagina for purposes of conjoining spermatozoon and ovum to achieve reproduction.*

Keep that sentence in mind.

Latinate circumlocutions were not the only device used to protect innocent young minds from naughty words. Their very orthography was disguised. To help explain this, here's a joke from the early days of aviation. It seems an old hermit was brought from his cave to civilization in the early years of the century. He was taken to an airport and shown many marvels that he had never seen — the telephone, the typewriter, the aeroplane. The old gent agreed to take a ride in a plane but he had a few questions first. One was about the funny symbols on the typewriter keyboard — for example, this one: *. He was told it was an asterisk. The old hermit sat and played with the typewriter while they warmed up the engine on the aeroplane. When they came to get him, they found this message: "I ain't flying in no durn contraption because I only got one *."

In addition to being a handy abbreviation for "ass-to-risk," the * is sometimes used to render bawdy words less offensive. Consider one of the more common Anglo-Saxon verbs: it used to be printed *f*ck*. Because the language has so few vowels, resourceful children who came across *f*ck* could experiment with the spelling: fack? feck? fick? fock? fuck? fwck? fyck? They knew the real word had to be in that list someplace! Because of this, the * was sometimes called upon to perform double duty as a consonant. As offensive as our more prudish forebears found the word *f*ck,* it wasn't considered the worst. Not by a long shot! The English lexicographer Eric Partridge published his authoritative *Dictionary of Slang and Unconventional English* in 1937. For nearly a quarter of a century, it was the only place where bright youngsters from genteel families could find out what those words actually meant. (After all, a guy couldn't ask his pals without admitting that he didn't know the meaning of words he had been pretending to have already *done.*) Partridge contended that the Anglo-Saxon for the feminine sex organ was more offensive in polite society than *f*ck*. For that reason, some writers doubled the asterisks, writing the word like this: c**t.

Let the kiddies try to spell *that one* by process of elimination! crit? cost? cist? Even an infinite number of apes would be a while hitting the right combination, with no way to recognize it.

Partridge's research, by the way, led him to conclude that the worst insult in the English language (at least circa 1937) was c**tf**e.

Here is our Latinate sentence you were told to keep in mind expressed in plain English using the asterisk. F*cking is when he puts his c*ck into her c**t and she isn't a v*rg*n anymore and maybe even gets pr*gn*nt.

The word v*rg*n got the movie *The Moon Is Blue* banned by the Legion of Decency in 1953. The terrible thing about c*ns*rsh*p (now *there's* a dirty word for you!) is that its self-righteous advocates tend to run amok. Why? That's simple—because the subject of sex tends to drive otherwise sensible folks bonkers, bananas, and haywire. There are loonies on the loose among us who would ban Salinger's lovely *Catcher in the Rye* from the nation's high schools because it contains the word *f*ck*.

That's silly. And sad. And scary. Fear of s*x has addled our judgment. But just to show how complicated a subject s*x really is, let's play devil's advocate for a moment. As repugnant as c*ns*rsh*p must be to all who love a free society, the c*ns*rs at least recognize that s*x is dangerous. Many of the pious pundits who've gotten rich during the last twenty years urging everyone to indulge in all the guilt-free s*x they could get ought to have known better. Rampant promiscuity has had some serious consequences—kiddie porn, snuff films, and pandemics of sexually transmitted diseases are only the most obvious. Bad writers fob off sentimental trash as adult drama by lacing their platitudinous dialogue with f*ck-this and f*ck-that. Reactionaries point to the porno shops on Main Street and streetwalkers of both sexes and all ages on suburban sidewalks to discredit everybody more liberal than Jesse Helms. A sex-saturated society consigns Gary Hart to political oblivion for hanky-panky with Donna Rice while continuing to worship at JFK's shrine.

We pride ourselves on having "outgrown" the sexual hangups of the Victorians without recognizing that we're still at least half-gaga when it comes to sex. Boy, oh boy, are we bluffing!

The ideal thing, of course, would be to temper passion with moderation, to eliminate superstition with education, to replace hypocrisy with sincerity, to abandon sham in favor of honest emotion. Yeah . . . *sure!* But this is *sex* we're talking about. American society can't agree — even in the face of epidemics of AIDS and teen pregnancy — whether to discuss sex in its schools or not. So, not surprisingly, we also can't agree on a common language to talk and write about sex.

Our generation has been lucky to have a sweet-natured moralist named Kurt Vonnegut write about important issues with wit and ingenuity. As a World War II combat vet and regular guy, Vonnegut was familiar with the salty language of the barracks and the locker rooms. Because he wrote in the vernacular, his books have been attacked by the letter-counters. Letter-counters are offended by four-letter words like f*ck, but they become *truly* enraged by seven-letter words such as *ssh*le, and they become absolutely apoplectic about ten-letter words like c*cks*ck*r or c**tl*pp*r. The letter-counters have plenty of political clout, too. The Federal Communications Commission has an official list of seven naughty words which must *not* be uttered on radio or television. As a society, we still don't trust ourselves to exercise good taste or good judgment when it comes to the language of sex . . . or s*x . . . or ess-ee-ex.

Since this is a book about sex (or s*x) (or ess-ee-ex), we have to decide what language is appropriate. After all, this scholarly volume might, like Gibbon's *Decline and Fall of the Roman Empire,* fall into the hands of a child. Given our long history of puritanism and our recent history of prurience, the book may well fall into the hands of emotionally immature adults. It isn't easy to achieve sexually mature attitudes in contemporary America. You won't find sexually mature attitudes in our schools or on Madison Avenue or in Hollywood or in the halls of Congress or in the tunes of Tin Pan Alley or on TV talkshows. When the subject is sex, we begin to snigger or swagger or circumlocute. The subject of sex still makes us nervous, jumpy, ill-at-ease, and self-conscious.

Sex is virtually a synonym for life. That makes it a very complicated subject. Few worthwhile sweeping generalizations can be made about it. The important truths about sex must be expressed in a language that conveys ambiguities, nuances, subtle shades of meaning, and dense layers of possible interpretation. The language of sex must be poetic enough for tragedy yet blunt enough for comedy. We won't include in this book any hard-and-fast rule about when f*cking is f*cking and when f*cking is coitus or copulation or intercourse or any of the hundreds of colorful or corny ways we've devised to describe this common activity. We accept the fact that the language of sex is like sex itself – unruly.

The Mechanics of Sex

What if your mother came in right now and caught you reading this? Wouldn't you be *ashamed* of yourself? Just imagine! A person of your intelligence and up-bringing, reading about "The Mechanics of Sex"! As if you didn't already *know* about the mechanics of sex! *Everybody* knows about the mechanics of sex. Yet each year hundreds of new books about the mechanics of sex are printed and swell the ranks of the thousands of books about the mechanics of sex that already clog the libraries and bookstores.

Unless you're under the age of six and live on the island of Tristan da Cunha without access to television or tabloids or any of the other blessings of modern civilization, you know about the mechanics of sex as well as you know that the sun rises in the east or that the ratio of the circumference of a circle to its diameter is 3.14, or thereabouts. You don't read books explaining that customarily the sun rises in the east or that the Greek letter *pi* is the symbol for 3.141592+, so why read an explanation that can amount to little more than the earth-shaking news that his little thing gets stiff and her little place gets moist and when the one is inserted in the other and frisked about a bit, it usually produces a pleasant sensation and occasionally produces a baby? So much for the vaunted mechanics of sex!

Ah, though! Sex is *never* that simple, not even at its most mechanical. Sex is almost endlessly absorbing. Its mechanistic aspects are inseparable from its spiritual dimension, being (as they are) the physical path to carnal bliss *and* the serial immortality of parenthood alike. Would you be embarrassed if your mother caught you reading a textbook about hydraulic engineering or liquid-waste management? Probably not. Yet many of us would feel ill-at-ease if Mom peered over our shoulder and saw us reading about "The Mechanics of Sex." Logic tells us that Mom could probably give Joan Collins a few pointers about the mechanics of sex, but the subject itself spooks us.

There are zillions of reasons why people keep reading thick, complicated books about this thin, simple subject, but one is especially worth consideration: we keep studying the mechanics of sex because the incongruity drives us crazy.

Incongruity?

Incongruity!

If the body is a temple for the soul, then the sex organs are part of the plumbing. The mechanics of sex *are* related to hydraulic engineering and liquid-waste management. Human reproduction is a function of ductworks, traps, and spigots. Sex is how we reproduce all that is wonderful within us, how we transmit our dreams via DNA, how we engage in the act of our deepest spiritual emotions. And we do this with *plumbing fixtures?*

Othello killed Desdemona, Don José killed Carmen, Romeo killed Romeo, and Juliet killed Juliet — over *plumbing fixtures?* No-no-no-no-no-no-no, that won't do. That simply won't do. A man and a woman cannot approach angelic ecstasy by temporarily connecting his faucet to her drain—can they?

Yes. Curiously and incongruously enough, ordinary human beings engaging in the commonplace mechanics of sex with their hilariously versatile organs can occasionally transcend mere pleasure to experience something that seems to almost give them a glimpse of divinity. This incongruity is mysterious, grotesque, funny, and interesting.

If you're *really* interested in the mechanics of sex, ignore all the spanking-new self-help books and, instead, bone up on the subject with the great classic of erotica, the *Kama Sutra*. This Bluffer's Guide (that you're reading) is a modest amusement written by a middle-aged couple in the boondocks for a publisher in the American Midwest—the *Kama Sutra,* it ain't.

The *Kama Sutra* describes in intimate detail a variety of positions for erotic shananigans that a contortionist would have trouble getting into and not even Harry Houdini could get out of. If you're *serious* about the mechanics of sex, run-don't-walk to your nearest decent (or indecent) library and get your hands on the *Kama Sutra*. Should your Mom catch you reading it, just say it was assigned in a course you're taking in Cultural Anthropology, Comparative Literature, Comparative Anatomy, or some such. Mom, being a good sport, will pretend to believe you.

A few salient points are worth making about our cultural mythology concerning the mechanics of sex. It seems reasonable to assume that nature is indifferent to how a spermatozoon is delivered to an ovum. Not so society. European civilization decided that the "normal" position for sex was horizontal—with the female on her back and the male on top of her. This face-to-face posture is now known as the Missionary Position because non-European tribes were amused and puzzled by the missionaries who preferred this position to the exclusion of all others. This obsession struck them as droll. It *is* droll. But cultural loyalties run deep in the unconscious. For people of European ancestry, the Missionary Position is normal and everything else is kinky. This was made plain in the 1981 movie *Quest for Fire,* an epic set 80,000 years ago. This film had real class—a special *gruntsprach* language was devised for it by literary high priest Anthony Burgess, while body language was created by that pop cult sage of anthropology Desmond Morris (he of *The Naked Ape*).

At the beginning of the movie (which won an Academy Award for costumes, even though they consisted of only a few skins—straight out of *The Flintstones*), Rae Dawn Chong is being serviced dog-style by Ron Perlman and Nameer El Kadi and whatever randy cave man takes a fancy to her, but by the end of the movie she's insisting that Perlman use the Missionary Position. Plainly, the moviemakers expect us to recognize that the Missionary Position represents at least one rung up the evolutionary ladder. Primitive peoples do it any old way, but civilized couples have the lady lie down on her back with the gentleman face-to-face on top of her (hopefully supporting his weight with his elbows so as not to crush the fair damsel). This is the only position endorsed by St. Thomas Aquinas.

Is that right or wrong? No one can say. It's purely a matter of opinion. *De gustibus non est disputandum.* If you want to use the scientific method to overcome your cultural predilection for the Missionary Position, you'll have to try all the positions and attitudes and stances in the *Kama Sutra* before venturing an opinion of their relative merits. (You must wonder how many positions St. Thomas Aquinas *tried* before making his endorsement.) This research, to be statistically significant, could take years. Decades. A lifetime. You might even fail to surmount your inbred cultural bias. You might, after all your energetic research into the mechanics of sex, conclude that the good old Missionary Position wins by a nose.

Masturbation

Masturbation is sex at its simplest. No courtship, no coy refusals, no headaches, no complaints about inadequate performance, no pregnancy, no divorce. As narcissism-in-action, masturbation is the ideal sexual activity for the Me Generation. Unsurprisingly, the sexperts are all enthusiastic about masturbation. Shere Hite puts the majoritarian view this way, "Masturbation seems to have so much to recommend it – easy and intense orgasms, an unending source of pleasure . . . perhaps in the future we will be able to feel we have the right to enjoy masturbation too – to touch, explore, and enjoy our own bodies in any way we desire."

In our tireless research, we couldn't find any contemporary pundit with reservations about masturbation. Gary F. Kelly, in *Learning About Sex* (The Contemporary Guide for Young Adults), a book that appeared in 1987 and was voted onto the Best Books for Young Adults List by the American Library Association, says that "there is also no such thing as 'too much' masturbation . . . there is no harm to mind or body, regardless of the frequency with which masturbation is practiced." This opinion was heartily endorsed by the American Society of Optometrists. According to Jay Gale, Ph.D., author of *A Parent's Guide to Teenage Sexuality* (1989), "Virtually all social scientists agree that masturbation is a natural form of sexual expression and that, other than the guilt inflicted by parental or societal admonitions, there is no danger."

Uh-oh! Just when it seemed a guy could flog-the-dog all the way to Nirvana, weasel words sneak in. *Virtually* all . . . *social* scientists . . . other than the *guilt inflicted* by parental or societal admonitions. Perhaps even now pulling-the-puddy is not 100 percent risk-free. If masturbation is such innocent merriment, why would parents and society *inflict* guilt with admonitions?

The answer, alas, is simplicity itself. Masturbation is a solipsistic sexual activity, but it *is* sexual and everything about sex is subject to taboo. Remember the trouble Jimmy Carter got into for confessing that he had lusted in his heart? Some folks believe that even *thinking* about sex is sinful, and those teenage boys playing whip-the-weasel sure aren't thinking about algebraic equations or inorganic chemistry.

In Christian theology, masturbation was the sin of Onan. If you look up *onanism* in the dictionary, you'll find it defined as masturbation or coitus interruptus. The biblical story is in Genesis 38. It's one humdinger of a yarn. Judah had three sons—Er, Onan, and Shelah. Judah arranged for Er to marry a woman called Tamar. So far, so good. But now it gets mysterious. "Er, Judah's firstborn, was wicked in the sight of the Lord, and the Lord slew him." What did Er do that was so wicked? We haven't got a clue. But we know what Onan did.

41

Judah insisted that Onan marry Tamar. Here's what it says in the translation calling itself the *Good News Bible*: "When he had intercourse with his brother's widow, he let the semen spill on the ground, so that there would be no children." This proved to be a major mistake (as well later proving to be a poor method of birth control). "What he did displeased the Lord, and the Lord killed him also." The death penalty for letting your seed spill on the ground. Masturbation as a capital offense. This is serious stuff.

The rest of the story in Genesis 38 is pretty weird. Judah insisted that Tamar wait to marry his third son Shelah when he got old enough. Meanwhile, however, Tamar disguised herself as a hooker and turned the trick with Judah himself, becoming pregnant and having twins.

In these few lines, Genesis 38 has enough sex for two weeks of TV soap operas and enough incest and mistaken identity on the highway to inspire a trilogy from Sophocles if he had known that tale instead of the one about Oedipus. The meaning of Genesis 38 is not entirely clear, but one thing *is* plain—what Onan did got him killed. Spilling seed on the ground was a high-risk sexual activity (so let's be careful out there). Perhaps this explains why generations of parents told junior that he'd go blind if he played with himself. And why generations of boys used the punch line from the old chestnut: "It's okay, Dad, I'll quit as soon as I need glasses."

Despite endorsement by virtually all social scientists, masturbation remains an area of confusion. In the movie *Meatballs,* one of the good-looking hunks from a wealthy summer camp is called a "jerk-off." His response is an indignant denial; he says, "But I *don't* jerk off." This raises the intriguing question of whether one can *be* a jerk-off with actually *doing* any jerking-off. The conundrum involves deep, philosophical issues about the nature of being, about essence and existence, and about whacking-off. While you wrestle with those deep issues, the plain fact remains that the expression "jerk-off" is an insult. Onanism has an onus to bear.

Despite all its good press, masturbation hasn't inspired many hit songs. The most obvious exception is Michael Jackson's monster hit "Beat It!" The advice in the title struck a chord with a large public. The thing is, though, that Michael Jackson is, well, a wee bit strange. The truth about Michael Jackson is weird enough for tabloid headlines with no fibbing. The guy lives alone with a chimpanzee. He goes to Disneyland all by his lonesome. He has cosmetic surgery. No wonder he sings a song like "Beat It!" Did Elvis sing such a song? Did any of the Elvises sighted hither, thither, and yon ever sing such a song? No.

Masturbation has fared better in literature than on Tin Pan Alley. It has it own literary magnum opus: *Portnoy's Complaint,* by Philip Roth. The book sold well, but it made readers nervous, too. There seems to be such a thing as too *much* candor about masturbation. The Kinsey Report said 98 percent of males admitted to masturbation (the other two percent apparently went in for prevarication or had their hands in a cast when the survey was taken). Kinsey caused rather more of a fuss when he said that 62 percent of females masturbated. Of course, he conducted his survey in Indiana during the late 1940s when they may not have had any better options, but the contention caused quite a furor. Many insisted that Kinsey's sample was atypical because only sex maniacs would talk with strangers about their sexual activities. If so, then 62 percent of the female sex maniacs in Indiana in the late 1940s practiced masturbation.

If you're interested in female masturbation, there are over fifty pages about it in *The Hite Report*. Of Hite's 3,000+ women respondents, 82 percent admitted to masturbation, and they describe how they do it in terms so graphic that the pages stick together.

Portnoy's Complaint, The Hite Report, and virtually all social scientists agree that you don't need to feel guilty about masturbation. According to one self-admitted expert, Betty Dodson, author of "Liberating Masturbation," "Masturbation is our primary sex life. It is *the sexual base* (her italics, not ours). Everything we do beyond that is simply how we choose to socialize our sex life." If Ms. Dodson is right, there should be no stigma attached to the label "jerk-off." Go ahead and *be* a jerk-off. You'll have plenty of company. Offhand, though, you might lay off if your eyesight dims.

SEX AND GENDER, SCIENCE, DIGNITY, MARRIAGE, AND MORALITY

> The little rift between the sexes
> is astonishingly widened by simply
> teaching one set of catchwords
> to the girls and another to the boys.
>   — Robert Louis Stevenson

Sex and Gender

What Robert Louis Stevenson called the "little rift between the sexes" has sometimes seemed like a great divide in recent years. One hopes that by now every sane and rational human being is committed to the principle of equality between the sexes. The *tension* between the sexes will persist. That's inevitable. The last decade of the millenium is a fine time to celebrate the creative tension between the sexes and delight in our potential to fuse them into that mystery we call "love."

We don't want for good advice. The French say, *"Vive la difference!"* Andrew Marvell said, "Let us roll all our strength and all our sweetness into one ball." Except as the stuff of comedy, the famous War Between the Sexes ought to end in an immediate cease-fire. (There are so many schmucks and psychopaths among the men and so many bitches among the women that some of us have been draft dodgers (and collaborators with the enemy) in this war anyway. The important issues of the moment transcend gender. Our immediate need is for broad-based coalitions to work toward a better life for the poor and homeless, a rebuilding of the economic infrastructure, fair play for the Third World, a lessening of environmental degradation, effective regulation of multinational corporations, a decrease in drug abuse, an equitable health care system, better schools and colleges, disarmament . . .

If we can lessen the little rift between the sexes, we'll have a lot more fun and a much better shot at addressing the terrible problems our so-called leaders have been ignoring or merely posturing about for so long.

Sex and Science

In vitro fertilization and gene-splicing hold the promise of making sex obsolete. In the past, only individuals could opt for the celibate lifestyle, but in the future whole societies could decide to do without sex. Science can take care of reproduction. When one considers how much trouble sex has caused—how many suicides, murders, nervous breakdowns, wars—it's easy to see the many advantages that a sex-free society would enjoy. Upon reflection, only one truly serious drawback comes to mind: sales of this book would plummet!

Sex and Dignity

Imagine yourself as the ideal sexual animal: savage,

virile, voracious . . . subtle as a shark, fastidious as a goat, and self-conscious as an alley cat . . . sound like you? Probably not. Most of the problems humans have with "doin' what comes natcherly" derive from our inability to treat sex as it's treated in the wild, as something natural. Our lives have become veritable onions of artifice—layer upon layer of pretense and delusion, layer upon layer of defense mechanisms and sham. Yes, there's still a vital animal at the core, potentially feral, but it's a domesticated beast—housebroken, timid, tenuous, guileful, worried about its self-image, and fretful about its precious dignity.

As long as you worry about your precious dignity, you'll have a lot of problems with sex. Sex involves spending some time with a person in everyday activities—chatting, watching a movie, sharing a meal, walking in a park—and then building up to a sensual frenzy that culminates in the removal of clothing and the frantic intermingling of various appendages of intimate anatomy . . . followed by the necessity of getting back into your clothing while carrying on some semblance of normal conversation. The positions, activities, sounds, smells, and gyrations of sexual activities cannot be conducted with anything like dignity—as dignity is commonly defined. Thus the inescapable conclusion: if you insist upon maintaining your dignity at all costs, you'd better enter a convent.

Sexual Morality in Fin de Siècle America

Tiptoe behind us into a real minefield—sexual morality. Most contemporary books about sex sidestep questions of ethics to focus on aesthetics – how to make the experience of sex more satisfying, more fulfilling, more beautiful. The unstated philosophy is, "If it feels good, do it." The promise is guilt-free sex.

In Western society, there's no guilt-free anything, sex least of all. Guilt goes with the territory. Guilt is the occupational hazard of having a European ancestry. Guilt is inherent in the Judeo-Christian way of looking at things.

The pundits of sexology are reluctant to appear to disapprove of *anything*. There's the usual hedge with the word "may," one of the more overworked of the weasel words. Then there's the vague matter of "established agreements for what people want from each other." Established agreements? About *sex?* Not even old-fashioned married folks in 1890 had "established agreements" about the kind of sex they wanted from each other. One imagines a scene in a lawyer's office as two sado-masochists bicker about the terms of their contract: "No, no! Every time *you* get to use the handcuffs and the cat-o-nine-tails, *I* get to play horsy for fifteen minutes with the Spanish rowels!" Face it, the pundits of sexology can't turn a fast buck in the sex-advice racket if they tell you *how* to do it on (or with) the one hand while telling you *not* to do it on (or with) the other.

Cole Porter said it best: "In olden days, a glimpse of stocking was looked on as something shocking, but now, heaven knows, anything goes!" *Anything?* Homosexuality – is it okay to do it with one's own gender? Incest – is it okay to make it with Mom or Sis? Adultery – is it okay to betray the marriage vow? Group sex – is it okay to do it with lots of strangers at the same time? Sado-masochism — is it indeed acceptable and safe for sexual partners who know each other's needs and have established agreements for what they want from each other? This sexual morality business is one gigantic bluff. We have no consensus about sexual morality, no semblance of agreement.

Some pundits confidently dismiss the very concept of sexual morality as a ridiculous vestige of our repressive past, a sort of psychic chastity belt, completely out of place in the modern world. Some of us, though, are left with lurking suspicions that sex is *not* that simple. Should a grown man have sex with a girl of 16? of 14? of 12? Should a grown man have sex with a boy of 16? of 14? of 12? Should a grown man take pictures of a grown man having sex with boys and girls of 16, 14, 12, 10, 8 and so on? Should a pimp profit from the sexual transactions of women bound to him more by fear than mutual advantage? When does friendly persuasion cease and date-rape begin? Pop psychology's attempts to de-sex sex, to geld the beast and render it harmless, haven't worked very well. Sex is still fun, still mysterious, still dangerous, still confusing.

So what sexual behavior is okay and what sexual behavior is *not* okay? How does anyone decide? Ah! With considerable difficulty.

Few people want to trade our contemporary sexual freedom for the repressive moral codes of the past. That said, we don't have any consensus on what ought to be done with the new sexual freedom. A glance at the sexual violence of all sorts around us suggests that we aren't doing very well as of yet. In the past, we tried to establish rigid codes of sexual morality based on natural law, canon law, statute law, and custom. All failed us. Lately we've tried to add a concept called "community standards," but that's too vague to be of much use.

Natural law is hopelessly irrelevant. We *are* animals, and as such we can learn a great deal about technique from life forms as diverse as the newt and black widow spider, but our fellow creatures get up to so many sorts of antics that in the end, their lessons must be considered too manifold for morality. Some animals will screw anything, while others mate for life and languish if a partner passes away. In providing an example of every form of sex, nature is naturally neutral.

Canon law offers perfect clarity, at least in theory. Each religious sect claims to know precisely which sexual activities are sinful and which are not. This is handy if you happen to be a devout adherent to a particular sect. The Methodist Marriage Manual, for example, used to be favorite reading matter among teenagers because its inventive suggestions for the creative use of stools and small stepladders in the marriage act were pretty spicy stuff in its day. Not even canon law is immune to rapid sexual change, however. Protestant denominations have been torn apart over the question of ordaining admitted homosexuals, and the Roman Catholic Church is having trouble convincing women among its laity to accept its decrees on birth control, abortion, women priests, and other matters. Not even celibate theologians can agree about sex these days.

Statute law is even more confused. One of the more comical instances of this chaos occurred not long ago when the police in the nation's capital decided to force a group of prostitutes to walk to Virginia during the wee small hours. The bizarre parade broke up when

the cops realized reporters had gotten wind of it. What they were doing was plainly illegal, an act of harassment with no statutory basis. Cops can't forcibly march folks they don't like to the next state. It hardly amounts to due process of law. But is prostitution okay? Is it okay anywhere, anytime? As a society, we don't have the foggiest notion. Municipal laws, state laws, federal laws amount to a crazy tangle. The Supreme Court doesn't know. Even when we try to pass laws in the few areas where we feel a sexual consensus exists (kiddie porn, for example), we fail to agree on wording that will please everyone. Why? Simple! Because when it comes to sex, Americans don't trust one another. Liberals suspect reactionaries of yearning to use police power to return us to the puritanism of Cotton Mather, while reactionaries suspect liberals of wanting a porno parlor next to every Sunday School.

In other parts of the world, there are umpteen churches to tell you that sex can be sinful and umpteen-plus laws to tell you that sex can be criminal—but confusion still reigns supreme. This is, in large part, because most people in most places in most epochs rely on custom to tell them what's wrong and right about sex. Custom might condone adultery among the rich, for example, even when it's condemned by canon and criminal law. Custom can also be harsh or lenient regarding homosexuality. Custom suggests an appropriate age for initiation into sexual activity. Custom is less rigid than law—thus potentially more humane, leaving room for some maneuvering, leaving room for some mercy. Custom does this because the wisdom of the people over time has taught us that sex *can* be very dangerous: jilted lovers, outraged fathers, cuckolded husbands, and raped women. When sexual passions are aroused, the potential for violence is omnipresent. Custom knows that.

Custom, however, is of virtually no use whatsoever when it comes to issues of sex in the United States. We are such a future-oriented society that we tend to ignore or scoff at the past, except as the stuff of nostalgia. This is especially true where sex is concerned because we preen ourselves on our superiority to our Victorian forebears. Custom is the stuff we brag about having defeated. Besides, in a pluralistic society like ours, we have too many customs—Italian customs, Irish customs, Mexican customs, Chinese customs, Jewish customs, Polish customs, Japanese customs. One has only to attend a wedding to see the continuing power of custom in general, but custom as a guide to sexual behavior is not much help.

Politicians trying to draft laws to keep prostitutes and porno shops in the slums "where they belong" have resorted to a new concept—"community standards." This vague notion presumably means that wealthy neighborhoods remain bastions of middle-class morality, at least as far as prostitution is concerned, while the slums are more sinful according to "community standards" because prostitution takes place there. This is amusing because it was precisely the Victorian solution: institutionalized hypocrisy by social caste, with wide-open red light districts in the slums and the surface appearance of sterling morality in uptown, polite society. This is the hypocrisy Stevenson depicts in his yarn about Dr. Jekyll and Mr. Hyde, the hypocrisy Wilde depicts in his picture of Dorian Gray. We have plenty of evidence that sexual hypocrisy is as alive and well as it ever was, with a slaveringly lascivious public ostracizing Gary Hart while spending billions of dollars on X-rated videos. If this community has standards, it's not at all obvious what they are.

Thus, most of us are left with the nagging fear that *some* sexual behavior may be immoral. Sex is so powerful that it hurts people all the time. Spurned lovers commit suicide. Casual lovers contract deadly diseases. Unhappy husbands and wives turn surly and morose, losing faith in themselves and in human nature.

The decisions we make can be difficult. Every one of us must at some point stop pleasing Mom and Dad and start pleasing a lover—a husband or wife, traditonally. Because we make mistakes, because we change over time, because we are not necessarily creatures who mate for life, we break up, we divorce, and we change partners. We even change genders. Sex is so tricky that with the best intentions in the world, we sometimes wreak havoc among our loved ones, and with the worst intentions in the world, we sometimes happen upon our One True Love.

All anyone can say with much confidence is that sex *is* dangerous—so dangerous that responsible individuals try to work out their sexual lives in ways that do as little damage as possible. This may mean that sometimes you ought to consider *not* sleeping with your best friend's mate, or not abandoning your children because somebody turns you on, or not sleeping with strangers. If that seems a bit straight-laced, old-fashioned, and fuddy-duddyish, so be it.

SEXY BOOKS

There is no shortage of books that fairly reek with sex. What the sexual bluffer needs are titles with a touch of class so that you can talk about sex without necessarily seeming to propose sexual activity. If the person you're talking with changes the subject to the international debt crisis, you can both pretend that you were talking about literature rather than sex qua sex. Here are a few titles which you can discuss without conveying the instant impression that you're a horny sex fiend. If you *are* a horny sex fiend, welcome to the club. You'll enjoy these books because they're fun to read.

Apuleius, *The Golden Ass*
This picaresque adventure has been delighting readers since the second century. Its central character is a licentious young man named Lucius, who blunders his way into metamorphosis and finds himself transformed into an ass. His ass's-eye view of the ways of the world provides lots of low comedy. If some of it seems old hat, remember that writers have been stealing from it for nearly two thousand years.

Honoré de Balzac, *Droll Stories*
Literary critics agree that Balzac was at his worst in his *Contes Drolatiques,* but what do literary critics know, anyway? This is the kind of stuff that made Balzac the *bête noire* of Iowa in *The Music Man.*

Giovanni Boccaccio, *The Decameron*

These hundred tales were written in the middle of the fourteenth century, and their medieval sauciness has kept them popular ever since. If you don't want to read all hundred, skip to days five, seven, and eight, where the stories are about love fulfilled and about unfaithful wives and husbands. The wives are especially cagey. One dupes her husband into cleaning an enormous barrel while she and her lover do it dog-fashion, with her leaning into the barrel, telling her husband to do this and do that. As a matter of practical advice, the episode won't help much unless your girl friend's husband happens to have a very large and very dirty barrel.

In another episode, the lover and the wayward wife convince the husband that he has an enchanted tree in his backyard. The wife gets hubby to climb the tree with her, and the lover begins to scream: "It's a scandal! Stop that! How dare you do those things with me watching?" The lover insists that he saw them making love in the tree while the husband insists that they were nowhere near one another. To show hubby the effect of the "enchantment," the wife and her paramour scamper up the tree and begin to screw like monkeys, all the while calling down to assure the husband that they are nowhere near one another. This gambit might work if your girl friend's husband has a big tree in his backyard. Perhaps husbands were easier to dupe in 1350? *Nah!*

Robert Burton, *The Anatomy of Melancholy*

This curious masterpiece is not for everyone; the bluffer who takes it up must know how to read. If you love language and admire erudition, this curious masterpiece will provide singular diversion. Most of the good stuff is in Partition Three, "Love-Melancholy." Burton was a scholarly clergyman who suffered from what we would today call a manic-depressive personality—in short, he was an emotional roller coaster. He seems to have conceived his book as a medical treatise on melancholia, as the condition was then called, but he got carried away by his own energy into writing a book about life and love and sex and scholarship.

Burton seems to have read every book written before 1621. His sentences bristle with quotations that pelt you like Henny Youngman one-liners. All that reading and study suggest that he was serious, yet his book frequently concedes that life is too absurd for serious commentary. Some of the ancient wisdom he tosses off, however, is shrewder than the pap you get from contemporary pundits, and quoting classical authorities about sex will make you seem smarter than you are.

In addition to reading about sex, Burton used to hang around the boatmen who ferried people up and down the Thames. Like today's traveling salesmen, they knew all the bawdy stories; the proper clergyman used to laugh until tears rolled down his face at the dirty jokes of the ferrymen. *Anatomy of Melancholy* was Dr. Samuel Johnson's favorite occasional reading. As one authority puts it, "Undeniably *The Anatomy of Melancholy* is one of the oddest, wittiest, and most learned books in English literature."

Stephen Crane, *Flowers of Asphalt*

Crane's first novel was a vivid portrait of prostitution, *Maggie: A Girl of the Streets.* After the huge success of *The Red Badge of Courage,* young Crane was employed by Hearst as a reporter covering the sordid nightlife of the Bowery and the Tenderloin. He was propositioned by a boy with eyes painted mauve and decided to write a novel about an innocent country lad sinking into degradation in the city. It's said that Hamlin Garland was so shocked by the first few chapters of *Flowers of Asphalt* that Crane abandoned the book. For that reason, you obviously can't have read it. However, you can talk about a book you haven't read. People do it all the time.

J. P. Donleavy, *The Ginger Man*

Get a copy of the unexpurgated version of this tour-de-force about an American in postwar Dublin. Once banned, it can now be read for the sheer fun of it, though there's enough sexy stuff to alarm the prudes. *The Ginger Man* was originally published by Olympia Press, a Paris firm that specializes in saucy trash but occasionally hits upon a real gem. Vladimir Nabokov's *Lolita* was published in the same series back in the bad old days of censorship. *Lolita* is also very funny, but its brilliant portrayal of sexual-obsession-as-love is so often misunderstood that one hesitates to recommend it. *Lolita* is not for sex bluffers but for readers who already love *Pnin, Pale Fire,* and several other of Nabokov's books.

James Joyce, *Ulysses*

Joyce's 1922 masterpiece was, in the astute words of Judge John M. Woolsey (the jurist who refused to ban the book in the United States in 1933) "a sincere and serious attempt to devise a new literary method for the observation and description of mankind." *Ulysses* is a sheer delight for people who know how to read; its stream-of-consciousness style is accessible enough. Sex bluffers, however, may want to skip 737 pages and concentrate on Molly Bloom's soliloquy (which takes up the last 40-odd pages). Molly's section has no punctuation, yet it's not difficult to follow. It's reputed to be the most insightful look into the female mind ever written by a mere male. If that's true, perhaps the two sexes can understand one another, after all. There's nothing aphrodisiacal here, as Judge Woolsey noted, and nothing emetic, either. As everyone knows, Molly concludes by saying "yes." If "yes" is what you want to hear (or say), Molly Bloom's soliloquy is an excellent topic of conversation.

D. H. Lawrence, *Lady Chatterley's Lover*

This novel was considered scandalous in 1928 not because it had graphic sex scenes, but because Lady Chatterley lowers herself with (gasp!) her *gamekeeper!* (Written today, it might feature Leona Helmsley making it with a doorman.) Lawrence seemed to consider love a religion and sex its central sacrificial rite. The notion that physical sex can be a path toward spiritual fulfillment is not new in human history but it made quite a splash in 1928 England. The Lawrence cult still persists in some academic circles where literary chit-chat is a required aspect of foreplay.

Henry Miller, *Tropic of Capricorn*

Henry Miller did the impossible in 1934. He proved with *Tropic of Cancer* that a book chock-full of graphic sex could have real literary merit. As literary arbiter Ezra Pound said, "At last an unprintable book that is fit to read." *Tropic of Cancer* combined the wiseguy sexual savvy of a New York City street kid with the literary ambitions of post-war Paris in a prose that owed a lot to Walt Whitman and a little to Céline.

Because it was well written, timid professorial types dared to defend it. But the book for the serious bluffer came out five years later: *Tropic of Capricorn,* the story of Miller's youth in New York. *Capricorn* is a much funnier book than *Cancer.* Besides, by talking about *Capricorn* instead of its more famous predecessor, the bluffer establishes credentials as one who scorns the obvious.

Anaïs Nin, *The Diary of Anaïs Nin*

For much of the middle of the twentieth century, *The Diary of Anaïs Nin* was the most famous unpublished work in the world. The confidante of many of the famous figures in Paris during the 1920s and 1930s, her diary was shown to those lions, all of whom proclaimed it a work of genius, the first real revelation of the female soul. The problem was that the diary was too huge to publish in its entirety. Beyond that, some of the celebrities were not entirely pleased by what Anaïs Nin said about them in her diary. As published, the diary leads one to suspect some of the best stuff must have wound up back in the vault. The *Diary,* however, does give an illuminating look at sexual attitudes among sophisticates in the first half of the twentieth century. And boy, she *sure* knew a lot of famous people!

Ovid, *The Art of Love*

These three books of elegiac verse provide mock-serious advice about love. The first two books advise the predatory male, the third the female. Ovid's tongue-in-cheek attitude toward the moral laxity of Rome did not please Emperor Augustus, so Ovid was exiled to the Black Sea.

Petronius Arbiter, *Satyricon*

Petronius was the original party animal when parties were parties. He became the *arbiter elegantiae* for the Roman Emperor Nero, the guy who decided who was "hot" and what was "not." According to the historian Tacitus, "The emperor thought nothing charming or elegant in luxury unless Petronius had expressed to him his approval of it." Tacitus was a prude who disapproved of Petronius, saying that "indolence had raised him to fame as energy raises others."

Petronius, the world-weary cynic, was in the perfect place at the perfect time to write his *Satyrikon Liber.* The episodes we have are our most brilliant examples of the vulgar Latin idiom, *sermo plebeius,* the dialect of ordinary folks as opposed to the literary Latin of Cicero and posh private schools. The most famous fragment tells of an orgy at the house of the *nouveau riche* Trimalchio, a pretentious dupe scorned by his guests. Happily, you don't have to be able to read to enjoy this picaresque farce: Federico Fellini did a movie version of *Satyricon* in 1970, a lushly opulent visual feast. If movies are the *sermo plebeius* of contemporary literature, Fellini makes an ideal *arbiter elegantiae.* Critics didn't know what to make of the movie, so pretend you got your Petronius from the book.

François Rabelais, *Gargantua and Pantagruel*

This sixteenth-century tale of giants is a vast exercise in high spirits. Much of it is sheer buffoonery. Obscenity is a major aspect of the humor. If the book has a philosophy, it's that "laughter is the proper passion of man."

Laurence Sterne, *The Life and Opinions of Tristram Shandy*

This is the world's silliest masterpiece. Sterne was an eighteenth-century Anglican clergyman, whose book consists of whimsical digressions, typographical gimmicks, and prurient innuendoes. Its obstinate refusal to take sex seriously is one of the best things about it.

Vatsyayana, *Kama Sutra*

The *Kama Sutra* is the classical text on eroticism from India, where they've been studying sex seriously for a very long time. Perhaps because there were so many of them, the Indians liked categories and systems to impose order on the chaos of life. Sex being life at its most chaotic, they organized it too. At least they didn't make the ridiculous error of the Puritans. Far from trying to curb sex, they set up a system which made it a proper goal of life (*dharma*). Because sexual intercourse was so important, they wanted it done right. *Kama Sutra* means "aphorisms of love," and it goes into great detail on technique. On one level, the book's a marriage manual about healthy sex, but it's more than just that. Vatsyayana adds a touch of Machiavelli to his Kinsey. He also has lots of hints for using sexual virtuosity to manipulate people. In addition, there's quite a bit of good exotic poetry that appeals to Western readers.

SEX IN THE CINEMA

Gibbon's task in summarizing the decline and fall of the Holy Roman Empire was a mere bagatelle compared to the task of summarizing sex in the cinema. Zillions of nubile starlets have jiggled and panted their ways through millions of steamy scenes. Not even Pauline Kael knows about every kiss-kiss and every bang-bang. What you, the bluffer, need is not omniscient knowledge of cinematic spice but a few choice items so that when browsing in the video store with a companion, you can select a film that has a touch of class. Sex is well-nigh ubiquitous in the movies, but classy sex is something else again. Here are a few titles to offer you a range of racy options.

Bringing Up Baby (1938)

This Katharine Hepburn-Cary Grant farce about a leopard and a dinosaur bone has no sex in it at all, but it's a wonderful movie. Lots of the best movies have no sex in them: *Mr. Hulot's Holiday, The Third Man, The Yearling, City Lights, The Clowns.*

Casablanca (1942)

The aura of misty romance and star quality around this one blinds the innocent to its cynicism — Bogie does just what he had stopped Claude Rains from doing — that is, he makes the girl sleep with him to get the exit visa (and then gives her the heave-ho and sends her away with her dull hubby so he can go off and have fun with his buddy).

Deep Throat (1973)
This is the one in which Linda Lovelace blows the whistle on Richard Nixon to Woodward and Bernstein.

Double Indemnity (1944)
Sex makes a sap out of an insurance salesman.

Everything You Always Wanted to Know About Sex but Were Afraid to Ask (1972)
Only the title of this madcap farce comes from the book of Dr. David Reuben – the rest is vintage Woody Allen madness. Critics have panned the movie as uneven and tasteless. So what? When it comes to sex, if you can keep laughing, you may actually survive with your sanity intact.

From Here to Eternity (1953)
This one validates the adage that the best movies come from good-rather-than-great books. In fact, there's nothing in the James Jones novel quite as powerful as seeing Burt Lancaster and Deborah Kerr on the beach. This is the only sexy scene in the movie, but it's enough when it's this good (the rest of the flick is pretty fair too). Frank Sinatra haters will love the scene where the Chairman of the Board gets pulverized.

I Am Curious Yellow (1967)
Considered shocking at the time, it now seems rather silly, but good-natured. This Swedish import was one of the first sexually explicit movies to appear in ordinary theaters so you can pretend to want to see it again as a historical curiosity.

It Happened One Night (1934)

Capra-corn at its best, with madcap heiress Claudette Colbert meeting cynical reporter Clark Gable and trusting their virtue to the sheet-thin Wall of Jericho.

Last Tango in Paris (1972)

This film used bloated pretensions and an even more bloated star to bring explicit sex from fleabitten urban porno houses to prim suburban shopping malls. A must for those who yearn to see the Godfather get it on.

Monkey Business (1931)

There's no sex to speak of in this Marx Brothers romp, but they do impersonate Maurice Chevalier.

Monkey Business (1952)

There's no sex in this one, either, but it did provide Marilyn Monroe with her most appropriate role.

Monsieur Verdoux (1947)

Charlie Chaplin's blackest farce is a "comedy of murders" about a mild-mannered bank clerk who turns Bluebeard, murdering women to support his sweet family. The theme is similar to Hitchcock's 1942 *Shadow of a Doubt,* but Chaplin's notion of the macabre is something else again.

The Poor Little Rich Girl (1936)

This is a typical Shirley Temple vehicle, with the child star running away from home and winding up in a vaudeville troupe. Novelist Graham Greene was successfully sued for libel when he said what everyone else was thinking—that little Shirley was sexy as hell. Greene thought it was because she always showed the legs of a woman beneath that innocent face. We found out from her memoirs that Hollywood moguls thought she was so sexy that they tried to . . . (yes, they really did try to).

The Postman Always Rings Twice (1946)

Lana Turner and John Garfield star in this schlock masterpiece about how sex can get you into a lot of trouble, and just when you think things can't get worse, love rears its ugly head and the weirdness runs amok.

Sex, Lies, and Videotape (1989)

This is the one about sex, lies, and . . . what was that again? Oh, yeah . . . *videotape!*

She Done Him Wrong (1933)

Mae West's best movie, based on her play *Diamond Lil.* This is the one in which she tells Salvation Army officer Cary Grant, "You can be had." When it comes to Hollywooden sex, Mae West is the acme and epitome.

The Shiek (1921)

This hokey, campy, racist, imperialist camel-opera made Rudolph Valentino the sex symbol (the Tom Cruise) of his sex-crazed age.

Swept Away by an Unusual Destiny in the Blue Sea of August (1975)

Director Lina Wertmüller's worst film was a huge success in America, perhaps because all the heavy-handed political allegory let viewers pretend that they were interested in more than the heavy-handed sex scenes. If you want to see a good Lina Wertmüller movie, try *Love and Anarchy* (1972).

A SHORT HISTORY OF
THE CONDOM

Not long after 1492, an epidemic of syphilis swept through Europe. Some experts say that Columbus and his crew brought the disease back from the New World; other experts say that it was only a curious coincidence that the epidemic began not long after Columbus' crew took shore leave. The new contagion was called "the French Disease" by everyone who wasn't French. Early in the sixteenth century, the Italian poet Girolomo Fracastoro coined the term "syphilis" in an epic poem on the condition.

The invention of the condom is sometimes attributed to the Italian anatomist Gabriel Fallopius; if not for the possible confusion, you might think of the condom as a "Fallopian tube." (Fallopius was the first anatomist to descibe the Fallopian tubes.) The condom of Fallopius was a linen sheath. It was not an immediate success. Madame de Sevigne expressed the common opinion when she said it was "gossamer against infection, steel against love." William Shakespeare had already written the quatrain you learned in grade school:

> In days of old when men were bold
> And condoms weren't invented,
> They wrapped a sock around their cock
> And that's how children were prevented.

The sock was not the only expedient. In the Orient,

condoms made of tortoise shell and leather were used. The word "condom" was coined by the dissipated poet John Wilmot, second Earl of Rochester, whose "Panegyric upon Condum" appeared in 1665. It's a portmanteau word combining the Latin *cunnus* (three guesses what *cunnus* means) with *dum,* a suffix meaning "it won't work." Dissatisfaction with the condom has achieved a certain respectability now that it stars in ads for itself on television.

GLOSSARY

Abortion – an issue we wouldn't touch with a ten-foot pole.

AIDS – Acquired Immune Deficiency Syndrome; the saddest acronym of our era.

Anal Sex – according to Burton's *Anatomy,* one poet calls this "sowing seed among the rocks." Johannes de la Casa says that it's a holy act, and he goes so far as to say that "Venus should not otherwise be used."

Candidiasis – an overgrowth of yeast fungus in the vagina (what Voltaire has to do with it is more than we know).

Cervical Cap – a little gimmie cap worn by peasants in the duchy of Cervica.

Chancre – a casino game familiar in Las Vegas and Atlantic City.

Chlamydia – STD with gonorrhea-like symptoms.

Clap – slang term for "applause."

Clitoral Hood – tissue from the labia minora that forms a hood-like covering over the clitoris when it wishes to remain incognito.

Cowper's Glands – Cowper's glands are nobody's business but his and Mrs. Cowper's. (Oh, all right . . .

two small glands that connect with the urethra in a male just below the prostate.)

Cunnilingus–the language they speak on the isle of Cunni.

D and C–the letters you use after Washington–if you mean the city, not the state.

Dildo–the sure cure for penis envy.

Douche Bag–a person with no charm at all, as in "Boy, is *he* a douche bag!"

Dyspareunia–painful intercourse.

Ejaculation–a sudden utterance; a pious ejaculation is a brief prayer to earn an indulgence.

Fellatio–what you give to get a head.

Foreplay–fooling around in the front of the ship.

Genital Herpes–incurable STD, causing blisters and sores in the genital area.

Glans–the head of the penis.

Glossary–glossary? *This* is a glossary.

Gonad–a tribesman who meanders from place to place with his tent and some sheep or camels.

Gynecomastia–temporary enlarging of breasts in 80 percent of boys going through puberty (as if they didn't have enough troubles with their voices changing).

Hobosexual–a fucking bum.

Hormone – what's the difference between a vitamin and a hormone? You can't make a vita min.

Hymen – a membranous fold of tissue partly occluding the vaginal external orifice in virgins; named after Hymen, the Greek god of marriage (even so, "Hi, men" is a dumb name for the thing).

IUD – one of those government agencies that doesn't work very well.

Merkin – a pubic wig; also the name of the president in *Dr. Strangelove:* Merkin Muffley.

M*ffdiver – slang for c*********.

Nocturnal Emission – an emission which is nocturnal.

Nookie – poontang.

Pelvic Inflammatory Disease (PID) – dangerous inflammation of the Fallopian tubes that can lead to sterility.

Pessary – a piglike mammal with long dark bristles, native to Central America (wait! that's *peccary*). A pessary is a vaginal suppository.

Premature Ejaculation – when you think about it, one way or another, most ejaculation is premature.

Premenstrual Syndrome (PMS) – physical and emotional discomfort which some women experience in the days preceding menstruation; has been successfully used as a defense in murder trials by the same people who insist that a woman's menstrual cycle has no effect on her performance in the workplace.

Poontang–nookie.

Prick–a nasty man; usually preceded by the word "real," as in "He's a real *prick*." (Not to be confused with *dildo* which is *not* a real prick.)

Pubic Lice–what the hoity-toity call crabs.

Pussy–a young cat; a kitten.

Quality Time–the rare few minutes that today's parents occasionally devote to their children.

Refractory Period–the interval of detumescence after ejaculation; the refractory period lasts several seconds in teenage boys and several weeks in older men.

Scrotum–pouch containing the male testicles; immortalized in the verse sometimes atttributed to Robert Browning: "When I saw the love words on my scrotum, I was O so glad that you had wrote 'em."

Smegma–the cheeselike mix of secretions and skin cells that can build up under a foreskin or around the lips of a vulva; smegma is a wonderful example of onomatopoeia–what *else* would you call the stuff?

Snatch–to grab roughly; *n.*, a burglary.

Sodomy–the favorite horseplay in the biblical city of Sodom (energetic research has yet to determine the favorite antics in its sister city, Gomorrah).

Speculum–the duck-billed medical instrument used to open and view the vagina during a pelvic exam (you always wondered what that dingus was called, didn't you?).

STD – sexually transmitted disease; not to be confused with STP or PTL.

Testosterone – the primary male sex hormone; often blamed for war, crime, the common cold, air pollution, and Geraldo Rivera.

Trichomoniasis ("Trich") – infection of the female genitals caused by a microscopic one-celled animal; males contract and transmit "trich" but seldom have symptoms (and isn't that *just like* them!).

Tubal Legation – embassy of the emerging nation of Tubal.

Vaginismus – female genital dysfunction causing muscles surrounding the vagina to go into involuntary spasms when penetration is attempted.

Vasectomy – surgical sterilization of males by cutting the vas deferens; this allows seminal fluid to ejaculate but not sperm; common side effects of the procedure include . . . no . . . you don't really want to hear about them.

VCF (Vaginal Contraceptive Film) – contraceptive method of using paper-thin, two-inch-square films containing spermicide, inserted in the vagina prior to whoopee (it takes a *very* modern Ms to entrust her sex life to VCF).

Venereal Warts – small genital bumps caused by a virus and spread by sex (as if AIDS and herpes aren't enough, we have to risk *warts* too? Ugh!).

Vestibule – entrance to a church, hotel, or vagina.

Vulva – reliable automobile from Sweden.

Zygote – the single cell that results from the union of an egg and a sperm despite the best efforts of condom, diaphragm, spermicide, sneezing, and prayer; zygote is not a very interesting word but an alphabetical list needs at least one entry under *Z* and what else was there . . . *zit?*

BIBLIOGRAPHY

If you're interested in serious, sober, earnest books about sexuality, here's a few good ones by smart people. With so little time to read, you ought to be reading Jane Austen, Lewis Carroll, and Flann O'Brien (whose *At Swim-Two-Birds* is one of the funniest books ever written) instead of more and more books about sex. If you can't learn what you need to know from the likes of Robert Coles and Ivan Illich, you may be a hopeless case, anyway.

Calderone, Mary S., and Eric W. Johnson. *The Family Book About Sexuality.* New York: Harper & Row, 1989.

Coles, Robert, and Geoffrey Stokes. *Sex and the American Teenager.* New York: Harper & Row, 1985.

Illich, Ivan. *Gender.* New York: Pantheon, 1982.

Kelly, Gary F. *Learning About Sex.* New York: Barron's, 1987.

Thurber, James and E.B. White. *Is Sex Necessary?* New York: Harper & Brothers, 1929.

Bluffer's Guides
CENTENNIAL PRESS

The biggest bluff about the *Bluffer's Guides* is the title. These books are full of information — and fun.

NOW IN STOCK — $3.95

Bluff Your Way in Baseball
Bluff Your Way in British Theatre
Bluff Your Way in Computers
Bluff Your Way in the Deep South
Bluff Your Way in Football
Bluff Your Way in Golf
Bluff Your Way in Gourmet Cooking
Bluff Your Way in Hollywood
Bluff Your Way in Japan

Bluff Your Way in Management
Bluff Your Way in Marketing
Bluff Your Way in Music
Bluff Your Way in New York
Bluff Your Way in the Occult
Bluff Your Way in Paris
Bluff Your Way in Public Speaking
Bluff Your Way in Wine
Bluffer's Guide to Bluffing

NEW TITLES

Bluff Your Way in the Great Outdoors
Bluff Your Way in Home Maintenance
Bluff Your Way in Math
Bluff Your Way in Office Politics
Bluff Your Way in Philosophy
Bluff Your Way in Psychology
Bluff Your Way in Sex

To order any of the Bluffer's Guides titles above,
use the order form on the next page.

AVAILABLE SOON

Bluff Your Way in Basketball
Bluff Your Way in Dining Out
Bluff Your Way in Etiquette
Bluff Your Way in Fitness
Bluff Your Way in Las Vegas
Bluff Your Way in London
Bluff Your Way in Marriage
Bluff Your Way in Parenting
Bluff Your Way in Politics
Bluff Your Way in Relationships

Get Bluffer's Guides at your bookstore or use this order form to send for the copies you want. Send it with your check or money order to:

Centennial Press
Box 82087
Lincoln, NE 68501

Title	Quantity	$3.95 Each
Total Enclosed		

Name_____

Address_____

City _____

State_____ Zip_____